PLAYS FOR PERFORMANCE

*A series designed for
contemporary production and study
Edited by
Nicholas Rudall and Bernard Sahlins*

GEORG BÜCHNER

Woyzeck

In a New Translation and Adaptation by
Nicholas Rudall

Ivan R. Dee
CHICAGO

Library of Congress Cataloging-in-Publication Data:
Büchner, Georg, 1813–1837
    [Woyzeck. English]
    Woyzeck / Georg Büchner ; in a new translation and adaptation by Nicholas Rudall.
      p. cm.
    ISBN 1-56663-449-0 (alk. paper)
    I. Rudall, Nicholas. II. Title.

PT1828.B6 A74513 2002
832'.7—dc21   2002073497

INTRODUCTION

by Nicholas Rudall

Georg Büchner was born in a time of ferment in Europe, 1813. He admired Napoleon and the revolutionary ideals of the Romantic movement. His father trained him to be a doctor, but when he entered university as a medical student he quickly turned to literature and philosophy. His youthful forays into revolutionary groups taught him how to write polemics. He wrote for the group, which he cofounded, called the Society for Human Rights. He was so deeply political at his young age that he had to deal with early ostracism and a flight to Switzerland. There he went to the University of Zurich and continued his studies as a potential physician.

Then Büchner began to write—first the novel *Lenz*, then *Danton's Death* and *Woyzeck*. He was twenty-four when he died of typhus.

This play, if you can call it that, is one of the most remarkable pieces of theatre that has come down to us. It is, to put it mildly, fragmentary. When Büchner died it was unclear if he intended these fragmentary scenes as a vision for a new kind of theatre or a mere compilation of notes for an orthodox play in three acts. But my instinct, as I have directed it and translated it and adapted it, is that it was a vision of a new kind of theatre, one that was not bound by the strictures of conventional space and time. Büchner's politics were revolutionary. He understood and felt for the underclass, but his great and revolutionary gift was to see that theatre need not be confined to the conventional Aristotelian unities. His tiny play is epic.

Unfortunately for the modern theatre, *Woyzeck* was lost for almost a hundred years. When it was rediscovered it changed people's thinking, stimulated new minds, and in its own way allowed Bertolt Brecht to flourish and *Angels in America* to become mainstream.

The twenty or more scenes that survive have no necessary order, though there is a fairly clear temporal progression. It is the director and the adapter's task to make their own dramatic coherence.

This is my attempt not only to capture Büchner's peculiar fusion of earthy dialogue, bizarre stream of consciousness, and surreal excursions into language but to provide a structure that will make *Woyzeck* a play that theatres can do in homage to a remarkable man. Apart from that, it is unbearably moving.

CHARACTERS

WOYZECK, an impoverished soldier
MARIE, Woyzeck's common-law wife
ANDRES, a soldier in the local barracks
DOCTOR
CAPTAIN
DRUM MAJOR, a local stud
SHOWMAN
SERGEANT
GRANDMOTHER
CHILD
MARGARET, a neighbor
FIRST JOURNEYMAN, essentially another camp follower
SECOND JOURNEYMAN, the same
PAWNBROKER

Woyzeck

In the dark there is the sound of the huge blow of an axe, then of the chopping of wood.

Scene 1

An open field or clearing in the woods. Andres and Woyzeck are splitting logs. Andres is whistling.

WOYZECK: This place is cursed. You know that, Andres? See that light green strip in the grass over there? Where the toadstools are so thick? A human head rolls down it every night. A man picked it up once . . . thought it was a hedgehog. Three days, three nights later he was in his coffin. *(whispers)* It was the Freemasons, Andres, oh yes I'm sure of it. . . . The Freemasons! Listen!

ANDRES: *(singing and chopping)*
Two little rabbits
Sitting in a field
Eating the green green grass.

WOYZECK: Quiet! Listen! Can't you hear it? Andres! Can't you hear it? Something moving!

ANDRES: Eating the green green grass *(cuts a log)*
Till all of it was gone.

WOYZECK: It's moving . . . behind me . . . underneath my feet! *(stamping the ground)* Listen! It's hollow . . . all hollow down there. The Freemasons!

9

ANDRES: You're scaring me.

WOYZECK: So strange. It's so quiet now. You don't want to breathe. Andres!

ANDRES: What?

WOYZECK: Say something! *(he stares ahead of him)* Andres, look how bright the sky is. Over the town. It's glowing so bright. A fire in the sky—and the roar of trumpets. It's coming this way! Let's get out of here. Don't look back! *(dragging Andres)* Quick! Don't turn round.

ANDRES: Woyzeck? Can you still hear it?

(Woyzeck returns to the space)

WOYZECK: Silence. . . . Nothing but silence . . . as if the world was dead.

ANDRES: I can hear the drums down in the camp. We better go back.

Scene 2

Marie's room. Marie is holding her baby at the window—she is with Margaret. The evening retreat is being drummed. The Drum Major marches past.

MARIE: Dum da dum. Dum da dum! Hear it, my baby? Dum da dum. Here they come!

MARGARET: What a man! Built like a tree!

MARIE: Strong as a lion. *(the Drum Major ignores Margaret and salutes Marie)*

MARGARET: I saw that. You gave him the eye. You don't do that very often.

MARIE: *(sings)* Oh soldiers are such handsome men!

MARGARET: Your eyes are still on fire!

MARIE: So what? Take yours to the Pawnbroker and let him polish them for you. If he can shine them up maybe you can pawn them for a couple of buttons.

MARGARET: Who are you to talk? The Virgin mother! I'm an honest woman. But you! You'd get into any man's pants—seven layers thick. . . . Leather too! . . .

MARIE: Bitch! *(Margaret leaves)* Baby baby baby. What's it to them? You're the son of a whore, you poor thing. But that wicked little face fills your mother's heart with joy. *(sings)*
Sleep my pretty one
Sleep my sweet love
Your daddy has gone
My poor little dove.

I'll sing to you my darling
All the night long
Till you sleep like an angel
To the sound of my song.

(knock at the window) Is that you, Franz? Come in.

WOYZECK: Can't. It's roll call.

MARIE: Did you cut wood for the Captain?

WOYZECK: Yes.

MARIE: What's the matter with you? You look all . . . wild and . . .

WOYZECK: It happened again, Marie. But it was bigger this time. Isn't it written "And there came forth smoke from the pit, like smoke from a fiery furnace"?

MARIE: Oh Franz, Franz!

WOYZECK: Quiet, quiet! I can see it all. The Freemasons. There was a terrible noise in the sky. Everything was on fire! It followed me into town. I'm onto something. Something big. I don't understand it . . . not yet. But it's driving me mad. What does it mean?

MARIE: Franz!

WOYZECK: Just look around you. Darkness everywhere. When God goes away, nothing is left. I've got to get back.

MARIE: What about the baby?

WOYZECK: Oh God. I've saved a little something. *(gives her a coin)* See you later at the fairground. *(he leaves)*

MARIE: Oh that man . . . everything plays ghosts on his mind. He'll go mad. Mind like a watch spring.

12

One day it will snap. Why are you so quiet, my baby? Are you frightened? Didn't even look at you. It's so dark. Like we were going blind. Just the street lamp out there.

I'll sing to you my darling
All the night long

The shadows. . . . Like so many ghosts in the dark. I'm so afraid!

Scene 3

Fairground. Lights. People milling about.
(the Child sings and the Grandmother dances)

CHILD: Nothing on this earth will last
All will fade
All will pass.
(repeat)

WOYZECK: A young girl sings. An old woman dances. Death and life. Pain and joy.

(a burst of raucous laughter from Margaret and Andres)

MARIE: People! Stupid people. They're stupid and that makes us smart. Or something. The world's crazy. But it's a beautiful world.

(a tent in the form of a scrim descends)

SHOWMAN: Roll up! Roll up! Ladies and gentlemen! See the monkey! He walks on two feet. Like a human being. He wears a coat and trousers . . . carries a sword. Art improving on nature. See the monkey!!! *(enter Drum Major and Sergeant and First Journeyman, who could be a lower-rank soldier)* He's a soldier. But that's not nothing. *(looking at the soldiers)* Lowest form of life if you ask me. *(the soldiers start to leave)* Not interested? Then come and see the astronomical horse. Favorite of all the crowned heads of Europe. He'll tell you all you want to know. . . . How old you are . . . how many kids you've got *(to Margaret)* . . . You've got diseases? . . . He'll give you a list of 'em. *(bustle and seating)* Hurry up. The show's about to start. Hurry on up. It's the profuckin' prologue of the profuckin' prologue.

WOYZECK: Wanna go in?

MARIE: I don't mind. Yes, there must be lots of things to see.

(They go in. She sashays across the stage.)

SERGEANT: Hang on a minute! Look at that. What a woman!

DRUM MAJOR: Jeeesus . . . you could get a whole cavalry regiment outta that one. A few drum majors too.

SERGEANT: Look at the way she moves. That's one helluva body. All that meat to hold onto. But she moves like a fish in a pond. Didya see her eyes?

DRUM MAJOR: Like looking down a well . . . or up a chimney. Hey, it's about to start. Go on in.

(the Showman takes their money)

14

MARIE: It's so bright in here.

WOYZECK: In the dark, black cats with fire in their eyes. It's a strange night.

SHOWMAN: Now! Watch carefully *(brings in the horse—a full puppet operated by the Doctor and the Captain)*. . . . The unique phenomenon of the astronomical horse. Show what you can do now. Show us your horse sense. Put humanity to shame. Ladies and gentlemen. This animal here, with his tail and four hooves, is a member of various learned societies. He's a full professor at our university. He's a specialist in riding and kicking. But that skill is a natural and *external* talent of understanding. Now *(to the horse)* I want you to think inside out. Show them what you can do when you use your *inside out* capacity of reasoning. Is there an ass present in this learned company? *(Woyzeck has become intrigued by the question and stands up. The horse selects Woyzeck as the ass by nodding.)* Do you see how inside out thinking works? That's equine-imity. Astonishing. This is no dumb animal I tell you. This is a person, a human being. A human being of the animal variety. Yes. An animal. *(as he says this he places a bucket between the horse's legs and the horse pisses violently into it)* That's it. Put humanity to shame. This animal's in a state of nature, you see. Plain and pure nature. *(to an audience member)* Having trouble in that area? Pee pee problems? Take a lesson from him, *(to Woyzeck)* ask your doctor. And the message is: Man, be as natural as an animal. You were made out of dust, out of sand, out of clay. Do you want to be anything more than dust and sand and clay? *(various responses)* Now watch this. How's this for academic talent? The astronomical horse can do arithmetic. *(to the Child)* But he can't count on his fingers. He doesn't have them. He can't express himself, he can't explain. In fact, he's a transformed human being. Tell the ladies and gentlemen what time it is. Have any of you got a watch? A watch?

SERGEANT: A watch! *(takes one from his pocket)* There you are, sir.

MARIE: I gotta see this. *(she gets up and moves)*

DRUM MAJOR: That's all woman!

(The Showman shows that the watch says eight o'clock. It's important that those present confirm the time vocally. The horse should stamp his foot seven times and then in the suspense stamp the eighth time.)

SHOWMAN: Eight o'clock! I ask you, is that not remarkable? Ladies and gentlemen, this amazing feat concludes the performance. Thank you all, thank you all. *(The horse begins to exit, the tent falls to the ground. Everyone begins to exit.)*

(The Drum Major and Sergeant watch Marie as she passes them. Woyzeck follows her. The Sergeant stops him.)

SERGEANT: Give the man a hand, soldier. *(Woyzeck helps the Showman with the horse and the tent)*

(The Drum Major takes out a pair of gaudy earrings and follows Marie into the woods. The Sergeant dismisses Woyzeck.)

WOYZECK: Marie! Marie! *(he runs out of the fairground)*

Scene 4

Marie's room. Marie is tucking the baby into its crib.

MARIE: The man told him to piss in the bucket and he did it just like that. *(she takes a piece of a broken mirror from inside her blouse and looks at the earrings she's wearing)* See how they catch the light! I wonder what they're made of? What did he say? Go to sleep, my baby. Close your eyes. Yes, that's it. Close them tight. Now keep still or the bogeyman will come and get you. *(sings)*

You'd better close the windows tight,
Or a Gypsy boy will come tonight.
And he'll grab you by the hand,
And drag you off to Gypsy land.

(speaking) They must be real gold. A little hole in the corner, a bare brick wall . . . that's all we've got to live in. A bit of broken glass for a mirror. That's enough for people like us. But my lips are as red as my lady's lips. She can keep her long mirrors and gentlemen kissing her hand. I have nothing. Nothing. . . . Hush little baby, close your eyes. *(she flashes the reflection of the mirror on the wall and says)* Here comes the bogeyman. He's walking across the wall. Keep your eyes shut. If you see him, you'll go blind.

(Woyzeck enters. Marie covers her ears.)

WOYZECK: What's that?

MARIE: Nothing.

WOYZECK: Under your hand. I can see it shining.

MARIE: Nothing. An earring. I found it.

WOYZECK: I never found a *nothing* like that. Two of them, too!

MARIE: So? What does that make me?

WOYZECK: I trust you, Marie. Baby's gone to sleep . . . look at him! I'll just move his arm so he won't get a cramp. His forehead's all wet and shiny. Nothing but work for people like us. We sweat in our sleep, poor people like us. More money, Marie. My pay and a little bit extra from the Captain.

MARIE: God bless you, Franz.

WOYZECK: Gotta go. See you later tonight. *(he leaves)*

MARIE: Oh, I'm a bitch. I oughta cut my throat. What sort of world is this? It's all going to hell and it's taking us with it.

Scene 5

Captain in his chair, waiting to be shaved. Woyzeck is all fuss and bother. Woyzeck brings in wood, sets the chair, sets up the shaving materials.

CAPTAIN: Slow down, Woyzeck, slow down! One thing at a time. You're making me dizzy. Stop rushing around like that. What am I supposed to do with the ten minutes after you're done? What use are they to me? Think about this, Woyzeck. You've got a good thirty years to go. Thirty years. That's three hundred and sixty months. Then there's the days, the hours, the minutes. What are you going to do

18

with all that terrible amount of time? Huh? Take it easy, Woyzeck.

WOYZECK: Yes, sir.

CAPTAIN: I'm worried about . . . the world. I'm worried about . . . eternity. It's a hell of a problem, Woyzeck, a helluva problem. Eternity . . . is eternity. . . . *Is, well,* eternity. You can understand that. But it's also *not* eternity. It's just a moment, Woyzeck. A single moment. It frightens me. The way the world revolves in a single day. I mean, what a waste of time! What's it for? I can't even look at a mill wheel anymore. I get depressed.

WOYZECK: Yes, sir.

(the Captain uses the shaving mirror throughout this scene—to look at Woyzeck and to look at himself)

CAPTAIN: You always look so tense. A good man doesn't look like that, Woyzeck. Not a good man with a clear conscience. Talk to me, Woyzeck. How's the weather?

WOYZECK: Bad, sir, bad. It's windy.

CAPTAIN: Uhh, yes, you're right. There's a huge wind out there. I can feel it. My back is tickling. As if a mouse was crawling all over it. *(slyly)* I'd say it's a nor'-souther.

WOYZECK: Yes, sir.

CAPTAIN: Hah hah hah. Nor'-souther! Hah hah hah. God, the man's stupid. Really stupid. You're a good man, Woyzeck. *(seriously)* But you've got no morals. Morals *are,* well, living a moral life. You understand that? That's what it means. You have fathered a child without the blessing of the church. That's what our military chaplain says. Without the blessing of the church—that's his expression not mine.

WOYZECK: Sir, God isn't going to care if we didn't pray just before we got down and did it. The Lord said, "Suffer the little children to come unto me."

CAPTAIN: What do you mean? What a strange thing to say! I mean what *you* said, not what *He* said. You're confusing me.

WOYZECK: Being poor. Do you understand, sir? It's money. Money. If you've got no money ... it's hard to get people like me into this world in a moral way. But we're flesh and blood, too. We have no luck in the here and now, or in the hereafter. If we get to heaven, I expect they'd put us to work. We'd be making the thunder.

CAPTAIN: Woyzeck, you have no concept of virtue. You are not a virtuous man. Flesh and blood. You brought that up. Hmmmmm. . . . You know, when I'm sitting at my window . . . when the rain has stopped . . . and I see a pair of white stockings . . . ankles flashing down the street. Ahhhh. Goddamn, Woyzeck, I feel desire then too. I'm flesh and blood, too. But my virtue, Woyzeck, my virtue. So? What do I do? I say to myself over and over again: you're a virtuous man. You're a good man. A good man.

WOYZECK: Yes, sir. I don't think virtue's my strong point, sir. See . . . people like me, we don't have

. . . virtue. We only have what's natural. But if I was a gentleman. If I had a nice hat and a watch and a warm coat and I knew all the proper words, I could be virtuous. It must be a great thing, sir, virtue. But I'm just a poor man.

CAPTAIN: Well, Woyzeck. You're a good man, a good fellow. But you think too much. You're wearing yourself out. All that stuff going on up there. You always look so tense. *(he gets up)* This conversation has totally upset me. You can go now. *(Woyzeck tidies up)* And don't run! Slow down, Woyzeck, slow down as you go down the street.

Scene 6

In the street. Doctor enters and attempts to sneeze. Woyzeck next to a wall, finishing urinating and doing up his fly.

DOCTOR: What are you doing, Woyzeck? You call yourself a man of your word? Is that what you are? Is it? Is it?

WOYZECK: What's wrong, Doctor?

DOCTOR: I saw you, Woyzeck, I saw you. You were pissing in the street. Pissing like a dog against the wall. I am paying you two groschen a day. And food! Ohh hoh. It's bad, Woyzeck, bad. The whole world is going bad. Totally. Completely.

WOYZECK: But Doctor, when nature calls . . .

DOCTOR: When nature calls! The call of nature? Superstition. Utter . . . disgusting. . . . Superstition!

Nature! Haven't I demonstrated scientifically and conclusively that the musculus constrictor vesicae is controlled by the will? Nature! Man is free, Woyzeck. Man is the perfect expression of the individual desire for freedom. And you can't even hold your pee in? That's deception, Woyzeck, deception. *(he paces back and forth)* Have you eaten your peas, Woyzeck? Cruciferae, you must eat peas, nothing but peas, Woyzeck. Don't forget! Maybe a little mutton next week. There's a revolution taking place in science. The whole thing's going to blow up sky-high. *(examining Woyzeck's old urine)* Uric acid, zero point zero one. Ammonium hydrochlorate hyperoxide. Woyzeck, you need to take another piss. Go inside and piss again.

WOYZECK: I can't, Doctor.

DOCTOR: Pissing against the wall! Goddamn it. I have it in writing. You made a contract! But I saw you with my own two eyes. I just stuck my nose out of the window. I was letting the sunlight play upon it in order to observe the scientific phenomenon of the sneeze.

WOYZECK: But nature, Doctor. . . .

DOCTOR: Do you have any frogs? Maybe some frog spawn? A few tadpoles? A snake or two? Vestillae? Crystatelae? Be careful of the microscope, Woyzeck. I've got some microbes under there. I'm going to blow science sky high. A few spiders' eggs? A couple of toads? Pissing against the wall! I saw you! *(pacing again)* No, Woyzeck, I am not going to be angry. Anger is unhealthy. It's unscientific. I am calm, completely calm. My pulse . . . my pulse is sixty as usual. And I'm talking to you with complete equanimity. There's no reason for me to be angry with you. You're just a man. Now, if one of my newts had died. But, Woyzeck, you shouldn't have pissed against the wall.

WOYZECK: Do you understand, Doctor? A man might be a certain kind of character, have one sort of way of being. But nature is something else. You see, nature's something.... *(clicks his fingers as he tries to think)* How can I put it? For example ...

DOCTOR: Woyzeck! You're thinking again.

WOYZECK: Have you ever seen nature when it's inside out, Doctor? Have you ever seen the sun stand still in the sky in the middle of the day and the world looks like it's going up in flames? That's when that awful voice spoke to me.

DOCTOR: You've a medical disorder, Woyzeck.

WOYZECK: Yes, Doctor. When nature ... when nature's inside out.

DOCTOR: What does that mean, when nature's inside out?

WOYZECK: When nature's out, that is when nature's *out*. When everything around you gets so dark you have to get around by feeling with your hands. When you feel that everything's falling apart like ... like ... a spider's web. When you feel something there but there's nothing. When everything's dark but the sky is all red like the fires of a furnace in the west. When ... *(he starts to pace)* When ...

DOCTOR: You're shuffling about, you're thinking on your feet like an insect.

WOYZECK: It's the toadstools, Doctor. That's what it is, the toadstools. Have you noticed the patterns they make on the ground? If only somebody could understand those patterns.

DOCTOR: Woyzeck, you've got a beautiful aberratio mentalis partialis . . . second degree. Fully formed, though. Beautiful. I should give you a raise, Woyzeck. Second degree . . . yes. Idée fixe, but no impairment of the faculties. You're doing your usual stuff? Shaving the Captain?

WOYZECK: Yes, sir.

DOCTOR: Eating your peas?

WOYZECK: Just like you told me, sir. And the money helps my . . . wife with expenses.

DOCTOR: Doing all you're told to do?

WOYZECK: Yessir.

DOCTOR: You're an interesting case, an interesting patient, Woyzeck. It's a beautiful idée fixe. You'll end up in the asylum, I'm sure. But bear up now. You're going to get another groschen. Let me take your pulse, Woyzeck. Hmmm . . . yes.

WOYZECK: What am I supposed to do?

DOCTOR: Eat your peas and clean your rifle. You'll get another groschen soon.

Scene 7

Marie's room. Marie and the Drum Major.

DRUM MAJOR: Come over here, Marie.

MARIE: No. Do it again. March around the room. *(he marches)* You're a bull! . . . and the fur on your chest . . . like a lion. No man like you. You make me proud to be a woman.

DRUM MAJOR: You should see me on Sundays. Feather in my hat. Regimental gloves. It's really something. The prince always says: "He's a real soldier—a real man."

MARIE: Is that what he says? *(goes up to him and touches him)* A real man? *(he starts to kiss her and she pushes him away)*

DRUM MAJOR: You're a real woman. Jesus. I wanna fill your belly full of drum majors. I wanna regiment of drum majors outta there. Come to me. *(He grabs her again. She struggles and tears herself away—she tries to slash him with the mirror.)*

MARIE: Let me go.

DRUM MAJOR: Oh you wanna be wild, do ya? Wanna be an animal? Then c'mon.

MARIE: Just try me.

DRUM MAJOR: You've got the devil in you. I see it in your eyes.

MARIE: *(giving in)* I don't care I don't care. It's all the same.

Scene 8

Woyzeck enters with ladders and puts them against a wall. He then leaves. The Doctor enters, climbs the ladders, looks at the audience, and speaks to them as though he were addressing his students.

DOCTOR: Gentlemen, I am here standing aloft like David when he looked upon Bathsheba. But all I ever see are the panties of the girls at the boarding school hanging out to dry. Now. We come to the important question of the relationship between subject and object. If we were to take one of those creatures on whose behalf I speak to you all, the capacity of the divine for personal affirmation quite clearly reveals itself. And when we examine its relation to space, to the earth, to the planets of this universe, if—I say again to you all—I take . . . *(he takes a cat out of his jacket or preferably in a bag)* if I take this cat and I throw it out of the window, what will be its instinct in relation to its center of gravity? *(shouting)* Woyzeck! Woyzeck! *(Woyzeck runs back in, the Doctor throws him the cat, and he catches it)*

WOYZECK: Doctor, the cat is biting me.

DOCTOR: And there you are! You're holding it in your arms as if it was your grandmother. You're an idiot.

WOYZECK: I'm shaking, Doctor.

26

DOCTOR: *(coming down the ladder)* Oh really? How interesting? How very very interesting. And what do I find here? *(inspecting Woyzeck's hair and eyebrows)* A new species of animal louse? Good one, too. *(takes out a magnifying glass and looks at the cat)*

WOYZECK: You're scaring it to death. *(runs out with the cat)*

DOCTOR: Animals have no instincts. At least scientifically. Therefore I shall use another subject to demonstrate. *(he flicks his fingers and Woyzeck returns)* Observe, ladies and gentlemen, for three months this man has eaten nothing but peas. Take note of the effect. It is patent. His pulse is irregular. Remarkably irregular. Notice his eyes. Note how strange his eyes are.

WOYZECK: Doctor, everything is going dark again. *(he almost falls down)*

DOCTOR: Don't worry, Woyzeck. A few more days and it'll all be over. *(he jabs at Woyzeck's throat and elsewhere)* The effect is visible, palpable, and scientific. Now, Woyzeck. Just wiggle your ears for the people here while we're at it. I meant to show you this before. He can do both of them separately. Do it!

WOYZECK: Doctor . . .

DOCTOR: Do I have to do it for you, you animal? What are you, a cat? Well, there you are everyone. Another case of progressive assification . . . a direct result of being brought up by females and the use of the German language. And you're losing your hair. Has your mother been pulling it out? Does

27

she want something to remember you by? No. . . .
Gentlemen! It's the peas, all of you, it's the peas.
Well, that's the end of the lecture. Thank you all.
When you've taken those things back in, Woyzeck,
the Captain wants to see you.

WOYZECK: Yessir.

Scene 9

*On the street. The Doctor is walking fast, followed by the
out-of-breath Captain.*

CAPTAIN: Doctor! Hold on a minute! Doctor! Not so
fast, not so fast. If you rush like that, the only thing
you'll catch up with is your last day on earth. A
good man—with a clear conscience—doesn't rush
about like that. A good man. *(He's breathing heavily.
The Doctor tries to get away but the Captain has him by
the coat.)* Grant me the privilege of saving a human
life.

DOCTOR: I'm in a hurry, Captain. I have to go!

CAPTAIN: You are a grave robber, sir. You'll wear your
legs off down to the bone. . . . You're a bitch witch
on a broomstick.

DOCTOR: Let me tell you something—your wife will
be dead within a month. Yes. Internal collapse
brought on by complications in the seventh
month. Twenty identical cases. All died. One
month. You'd better get used to the idea.

CAPTAIN: Doctor, please stop—I get so depressed. I keep imagining things: I see my coat hanging on the wall with nobody in it and I burst into tears.

DOCTOR: Hmmmm. Puffy . . . obese . . . fat neck . . . prone to apoplexy, no doubt. Yeeeees, Captain . . . that's the way you'll go. Definitely an aneurism . . . seizure of the brain. The stroke may only affect one side, of course . . . semi-paralysis. You'd still be able to move the other half. You might be lucky. It could be local cerebral paralysis. Then you'd be a sort of human rutabaga. Yes. That's my diagnosis. Four weeks. Now there is the outside chance that you could become a really interesting case. It's possible that just half your tongue could become paralyzed. If that occurs, I could do some experiments that would put your name in the annals of medical history.

CAPTAIN: Don't frighten me, Doctor. People can die of fright—sheer goddamn fright. I can see them now . . . my mourners, my friends . . . with onions in their pockets to make them cry. But they will say, "He was a good man, a good man." You bastard! You're a nail in my coffin!

DOCTOR: (he takes off his hat) See this? Empty! No brain!

CAPTAIN: (pointing to a button on his jacket) . . . that's a piece of bone—you're a bonehead. No offense, no offense. I am a virtuous man, but if you trifle with me I can give as good as I get. If I want to . . . if I want to. . . .

(Woyzeck enters walking down the street)

CAPTAIN: Hey, Woyzeck! Where you running off to? Hold it a minute! Hold it! You run through this world like a barber with an open razor. One of these days you'll give someone a really nasty cut. You're running around as if you had to shave a regiment of eunuchs. Miss one long hair and you'll be strung up. One long hair . . . a hair . . . what was it I wanted to say, Woyzeck? What made me think of beards?

DOCTOR: Pliny remarks that the wearing of facial hair by the *military* ought to be discouraged. . . .

CAPTAIN: Ah yes . . . this beard problem. Tell me, Woyzeck, have you found a hair in your soup recently? I don't think he gets it. A hair . . . Woyzeck . . . from someone's moustache . . . an engineer say . . . a sergeant . . . a drum major? Well, Woyzeck? But he's got a good wife . . . she's not like all the rest of them.

WOYZECK: Yes, sir. What do you mean, sir?

CAPTAIN: Look at his face! Well maybe not in his soup—but if he pops round the corner he might find that hair sticking to a certain pair of lips. A certain pair of lips, Woyzeck. Oh yes, I know what love is too, Woyzeck. Look at him . . . he's white as chalk.

WOYZECK: Captain, sir, I'm just a poor man. She's all I've got in the world. Please, sir—don't make jokes—please, sir.

CAPTAIN: Make jokes? Me? Make jokes?

DOCTOR: Your pulse, Woyzeck! It's quick, it's skipping, it's violent and irregular.

WOYZECK: The earth is hotter than the fires of hell, sir, and I'm as cold as ice. Ice! Hell is cold, I'll bet you. *No not her!* I don't believe it, I don't believe it!

CAPTAIN: Stop looking at me like that! You want a couple of bullets in your brain? Your eyes are like a pair of knives. Stop it! I'm only trying to help 'cause you're a good man, Woyzeck, a good man.

DOCTOR: Facial muscles taut, rigid. The occasional twitch. Physically tense, excitable.

WOYZECK: I'm going. Anything's possible. Slut! Bitch! Anything! Nice day, Captain. Sky's beautiful—cold, gray, hard. You could hammer a nail into it and hang yourself from the sky. It's all because of a little pause between the words "yes" and "yes" again and "no." Yes and no, Captain. Did the no lead to the yes or the yes to the no? I'll have to think about that. *(he leaves, slowly at first, then faster and faster)*

DOCTOR: You're a unique phenomenon, Woyzeck! You're going to get a raise! Woyzeck! *(running after him)*

CAPTAIN: People! They make me dizzy. Look at them! One scuttling away like a long-legged spider—the other chasing his shadow. Thunder after lightning. Grotesque! Grotesque! But I'm not like that. I'm no fool. A good man, a good man.

31

Scene 10

Marie's room. Woyzeck is staring hard at her.

WOYZECK: I can't see it! I can't see it! My God, why can't I see it? It should be there. Why can't I grab it in my hands?

MARIE: Franz? Franz! What's the matter? You're acting crazy, Franz.

WOYZECK: A sin so fat . . . and thick and big. It stinks so high the angels will fall out of heaven. You have a red mouth, Marie. Pure as sin. Not a scab on it. How can sin be so beautiful?

MARIE: *(touching his forehead)* Are you hot, Franz? A fever? Is that what's making you act so crazy?

WOYZECK: Goddamn you! Is this where he stood? Was he here standing here like this, like this?

MARIE: The days are long and the world grows old. A lot of people can stand here or anywhere, one after the other. Why are you looking at me like that? You're scaring me to death.

WOYZECK: Nice street out there. You can walk about . . . wear your feet down to the bone. Walking around, meeting people.

MARIE: Meeting people?

WOYZECK: A lot of people pass by here . . . on this street. Don't they? You can talk to them. Whoever you want. Got nothing to do with me. Him. Right here. Should've been me.

MARIE: Him? Who are you talking about? I'm supposed to tell people to keep off the streets? Muzzle 'em like dogs?

WOYZECK: Your lips are so beautiful, Marie. So red. You should have left them at home. But that would have brought the wasps in.

MARIE: What's bugging you? You're like a cow chased by your goddamn wasps.

WOYZECK: I saw him!

MARIE: You can see a lot of things when the sun's out 'n you've got two eyes.

WOYZECK: *(he goes after her)* SLUT!

MARIE: *(she slashes at him with the mirror)* Don't you touch me, Franz! You can stick a knife in my guts but don't touch me. Not like that. My own father was afraid to touch me after I was ten years old. He didn't touch me after I was ten years old. I just looked into his eyes and he couldn't do it.

WOYZECK: Whore! *(she tentatively leaves but lingers)* No! It should show, it should show! Every man is an abyss. When you look down you get dizzy. It should show! *(looking at her and the baby)* But she looks like innocence itself. But innocence with a stain on her body. *(she runs away)* But I can't really know . . . or prove . . . how can you be sure?

Scene 11

Andres is cleaning his rifle. Sings.

ANDRES: Our landlord has a pretty wife.
She sits in the garden all day long.
Sits in the garden waiting.

WOYZECK: Andres!

ANDRES: What?

WOYZECK: It's nice out.

ANDRES: Yes. Sunday weather. *(continues to clean)*
There's going to be some music later. Outside the
village. Most of the women are up there already.
Nice hot night for a piece of skirt. They'll all be
sweating like pigs.

WOYZECK: Dancing, Andres. They'll be dancing.

ANDRES: Yeah. At the Horse and Star.

WOYZECK: Dancing. Dancing.

ANDRES: Yeah. *(oblivious)* Why not?
Till the tall town clock strikes twelve
She sits in the garden wa-iting.
With an eye on all the so-oldiers.

WOYZECK: Andres, I can't get any rest. Can't stop
thinking.

ANDRES: Don't be stupid.

WOYZECK: I've got to get out of here. Everything is spinning around. Dancing, dancing. Their hands will be hot. Damn her, Andres. Damn her.

ANDRES: What's the matter with you?

WOYZECK: Got to go.

ANDRES: She's not worth it, Franz.

WOYZECK: Got to get out. It's so hot in here. *(leaves)*

ANDRES: *(under his breath)* Whore.

Scene 12

The tavern. In the interest of economy, the First Journeyman could be the Sergeant. He and the Second Journeyman enter very drunk, singing, and starting a halfhearted fight.

FIRST JOURNEYMAN: *(sings)* I've got a shirt on,
Don't know whose.
My whole darn soul
Just stinks of booze.

(they begin to fight)

SECOND JOURNEYMAN: How about a punch in the mouth? My friend, my brother, my . . . Make a hole in your soul. I'm all muscle. *(shadowboxes)* One punch, one dead flea. *(continues)* One and one and one and one.

FIRST JOURNEYMAN: It *does* stink. My whole goddamn soul stinks of booze. Everything stinks. Rots.

Money stinks. Rots. *(to the Grandmother and the Child)* But the world is beautiful. Why? I could weep for it. Weep till the beer barrels were full of my tears. *(pointing to his eyes and nostrils)* You see these? Think of them as bottles of booze. We could pour them down our throats. Tears of beer. Unlimited supply. *(everyone sings and people begin to dance)*

ALL: Two hunters from the Rhine
Riding through the forest so fine,
Talley ho! Talley ho! Talley ho!
Roaming through the wild woods free,
It's the hunter's life for me!

(Woyzeck enters)

WOYZECK: Him. Her. On and . . .

MARIE: On and on.

DRUM MAJOR: Round and round.

(the dance freezes as Woyzeck in an isolated spot speaks these lines)

WOYZECK: On and on and round and on and on and round. Spin. Turn. Sweat. Stop the earth spinning, God! Put out the sun! Just the dark! The dark that hides the lust, the bodies in the dark, man and woman. Man and man. Man and animal . . . animan. But. They'd do it in the sun, too. They'd do it on the back of our hands. Like flies. Sparrows. They'd do it anywhere. Look at her sweat. Hot. Bitch. Hot. On and on. And round and on. Look at the bastard. Hands—on her body—up her—in her. *(silence)* As—once—I—did. *(he starts to leave and is tripped)*

36

FIRST JOURNEYMAN: *(Affects the posture of a Southern Baptist preacher. Places his foot on Woyzeck and keeps him down during this mock sermon.)* Brothers and sisters! Our sermon for today is . . . Think upon the Wanderer. The Wanderer stands poised against the Stream of Time. And, cradled in the wisdom of God, the Wanderer asks—Why doth man exist? But, verily, verily, I say unto you. . . . How could the soldier, the tailor, the candlestick-maker survive, *exist* if God hadn't created man? Clothes, for example. If God hadn't created *shame,* embarrassment—*No skirts.* No trousers. So . . . NO TAILORS . . . Death, for example. If men didn't feel the need to *self-destruct* . . . NO SOLDIERS. Therefore I say unto ye. Do not despair. It is good. I looked upon it and it was *good.* But all is vanity saith the preacher. Money rots. All is vanity. So . . . in conclusion, brothers and sisters. Let's take a piss. In the shape of a cross. So a Jew will die. *(they hover over Woyzeck, ready to urinate on him)*

Scene 13

In the barracks—but given the cinematic quality of the text at this point it could be anywhere.

WOYZECK: *(on the ground, listening)* On and on. Forever. . . . On. On. No more music—SHHH! Quiet. *(on the ground)* I'm listening. Louder! Louder! Stab! Stab! Stab the bitch to death. *(silence)* Should I? Must I? *(wind)* I hear it in the wind. Everywhere. On and on and round and . . . stab her. Louder! Stab her. Death. Yes. Death. Yes. DEAD. *(waking Andres)* Andres! Andres! I can't sleep. Everything starts spinning when I shut my eyes. I can hear the music—playing on and on and on and round.

Then in the darkness, from the stones, a voice says . . . can't you hear it?

ANDRES: Yeah. Leave 'em be. Let 'em dance. People get tired. Quiet. God bless us.

WOYZECK: It's always the same. . . . Stab. Stab. I feel it . . . here between my eyes. Like a knife.

ANDRES: Go to bed, for God's sake. Take a shot of brandy. Put a powder in it. That'll do the trick.

Scene 14

At the inn.

DRUM MAJOR: *(to self)* Like a goddamn lion. I'm a man. *(to anyone)* You hear me? If you're not as pissed as Jesus at the Last Supper. . . . Leave me alone. I'll stick your nose up your ass. *(to Woyzeck who has just entered)* Have a drink. *(silence)* D-r-i-n-k. *(when Woyzeck ignores him, he pours the drink down his mouth)* Suck it in. Al-co-hol. I wish everything was al-co-hol. I said: drink. You—drink.

WOYZECK: *(whistles the hunters' song)*

DRUM MAJOR: You bastard! You tongue sucker. I'm gonna pull it out, tear it out, and stick it up your ass. *(Beats up Woyzeck. During fight he speaks.)* Bastard! Piss artist. You wanna whistle? Try it. Try it. Fight. Not enough breath for an old woman's fart. You want more? *(Woyzeck is bleeding)* Try whistling now. *(People try to pick Woyzeck up. Drum Major sings something in the background.)*

FIRST JOURNEYMAN: Jesus! Look at his eyes!

GRANDMOTHER: *(touches him)* He's bleeding.

WOYZECK: One thing after another.

Scene 15

In the barracks.

WOYZECK: Did he say anything?

ANDRES: He was with some friends.

WOYZECK: What'd he say? *(silence)* What'd he say?

ANDRES: What's the difference? What did you expect him to say? Nice piece of skirt. Wet as a fish and twice as warm?

WOYZECK: I see. So that's what he said. What was I dreaming about last night? A knife. Stupid things, dreams.

ANDRES: Where are you going?

WOYZECK: Got to bring some wine for my officers. You know, Andres, there was nobody like her!

ANDRES: Who?

WOYZECK: Doesn't matter. See you.

Scene 16

At the pawn shop.

WOYZECK: *(returning a gun)* Too much.

PAWNBROKER: Do you want it or not?

WOYZECK: How much is the knife?

PAWNBROKER: This one? It's a nice one. Straight. You wanna cut your throat with it? Well? You wan' it or not? I'll sell it to you cheap. For you, cheap. For everybody else, cheap. Cheap like your death, huh? But not free. No sir. Well? You wan' it or not? You'll have an economical death.

WOYZECK: This can cut more than just bread.

PAWNBROKER: Two groschen.

WOYZECK: Here! *(gives him the groschen)*

PAWNBROKER: Here! Here! Like it was nothing. But it's money! Dog!

Scene 17

Marie's room. Grandmother is talking to the Child. Marie reads the Bible and holds a crucifix.

MARIE: "And no guile is found in his mouth." My God, my God. Don't look at me. "And the Scribes and Pharisees brought unto him a woman taken in adultery, and set her in the midst. And Jesus said unto her: 'Neither do I condemn thee. Go and sin

40

no more.'" *(tries to pray)* I can't. God—give me the strength to pray.

GRANDMOTHER: *(to Child)* This one has a golden crown . . . he's our lord the king.

(Margaret sings to the baby)

MARIE: The child is like a knife in my heart.

GRANDMOTHER: Tomorrow. I'll go get the queen's little baby.

MARIE: And Franz doesn't come home. Yesterday. Today.

GRANDMOTHER: Blood sausage says . . . come on liver sausage . . . I've got a big sharp knife.

MARIE: Still doesn't come. It's so hot.

GRANDMOTHER: And I'm going to cut you up in thin little slices.

MARIE: "And she stood at his feet weeping and began to wash his feet with tears and did wipe them with the hairs of her head and kissed his feet and anointed them with an ointment."

GRANDMOTHER: Little slices.

MARIE: *(striking her breast)* Dead. It's all dead. O dear Lord. If only I could anoint your feet.

Scene 18

Woyzeck is emptying a box which contains all his belongings.

WOYZECK: This jacket is not part of the uniform, Andres. You might be able to use it . . . ? The crucifix belongs to my sister. And this little ring. Got a holy picture too. Here somewhere. Two hearts in gold. It was my mother's. She had it in her Bible. Um . . . it says: "Christ, As Thy heart was cleft and wounded, so let mine be. In Thy grace may pain be my reward." She's got no feeling left in her hands. My mother. Only when the sun warms them. Doesn't matter.

ANDRES: Yeah.

WOYZECK: *(reads a piece of paper)* Friedrich Johann Franz Woyzeck. Rifleman. Regiment, Second Fusiliers. Battalion, Second. Company, Fourth. Born . . . *(to self)* the Feast of the Annunciation. I'm thirty years old. Thirty years, two months, twelve days.

ANDRES: You don't look so good, Franz. You should report sick. Take that brandy with the powder, huh? Kill the fever.

WOYZECK: You know, Andres, when they make the coffins they don't know who's going to be in them.

(he closes the box)

Scene 19

WOYZECK: *(laying knife in a hole)* Thou shalt not kill.
Lie there. *(leaves quickly)*

Scene 20

MARGARET: *(singing with children and Grandmother in Marie's house)*
The sun shines bright on Candlemas.
The fields are golden grain.
And two by two we dance along,
Down the country lane. Oh pipers, play.
And fiddlers too.
Fiddle and play
Till your cheeks are red.

CHILD: *(goes to Marie)* Sing with us!

MARIE: No. Leave me alone!

CHILD: Please sing with us.

MARIE: I said leave me alone.

GRANDMOTHER: That's enough.

MARGARET: What are you doing?

CHILD: She started it.

GRANDMOTHER: *(to Marie)* Sing for us.

MARIE: No.

CHILD: Why?

MARIE: Because.

CHILD: Why because?

MARIE: Because.

MARGARET: Come over here. *(to the Child and then to the Grandmother)* Tell them a story.

GRANDMOTHER: All right. Once upon a time there was a little boy. He was very poor. And he had no father and mother. Everything was dead. The whole world was dead. There was nobody left in the whole world. And so the little boy started to look around. He was very frightened. He searched and searched. Day and night. But there was nothing. Nobody was left. So he decided to go up to heaven, because the moon shone down upon him with such a friendly smile. Up he went. Up and up. But when he got there, he found that the moon was only a lump of rotten wood. And so on he went, up to the sun. And when he got there, he found that the sun was just a dead sunflower head. So, up to the stars. And when he got there, what did he find? The stars were just little dead bugs, dead bugs stuck on some flypaper. So back to earth he came. And what did he find? The earth was just a broken, cracked pot. Empty and dead. So he was all alone. And he sat down. And he cried and cried and cried. And he's sitting there now. All alone.

WOYZECK: *(offstage)* Marie!

MARIE: What do you want?

WOYZECK: We've got to go. It's time!

44

MARIE: Go where?

WOYZECK: What's the difference?

GRANDMOTHER: *(to Child in arms)* Cut you up into little pieces.

WOYZECK: *(crosses to them)* My son. Christian.

GRANDMOTHER: Little pieces.

WOYZECK: *(tries to touch Child, there is a scream)* My God.

GRANDMOTHER: Little pieces.

WOYZECK: Christian, you'll get a hobbyhorse. Buy him one with this. *(gives two groschen to Grandmother, who cackles and then is silent)*

WOYZECK: Hop! Horsey horsey hop.

GRANDMOTHER: *(as they leave)* Hop, horsey. Horsey hop.

Scene 21

In the woods where Woyzeck left the knife.

MARIE: The town is back that way. It's so dark.

WOYZECK: Let's stay here. Sit down.

MARIE: I've got to get back.

WOYZECK: Your feet won't be tired. I promise you.

MARIE: What's the matter with you?

WOYZECK: Do you know how long it's been, Marie?

MARIE: Two years, come Easter.

WOYZECK: Do you know how long it's going to be, Marie?

MARIE: I've got to go. Got to make supper.

WOYZECK: Are you cold, Marie? No, you're warm. Hot. Hot lips. Hot breath. The hot breath of a whore! I'd move heaven and earth for one more kiss. Once you're cold, you don't feel the weather anymore. The cold dew of the morning doesn't touch you.

MARIE: What are you talking about?

WOYZECK: Nothing.

MARIE: Look how red the moon is tonight.

WOYZECK: Like blood on steel.

MARIE: What do you mean? Franz, you look so pale. *(Woyzeck pulls out the knife)* No! Franz! No! Wait! For God's sake. Help me. Help me.

WOYZECK: There! There! There! Why don't you die? Die! Not yet? *(cuts her throat)* Now? Now? Now! Dead, dead.

Scene 22

Voices offstage.

FIRST JOURNEYMAN: Did you hear it?

SECOND JOURNEYMAN: What?

GRANDMOTHER: Like the sound of death.

SERGEANT: There is a mist everywhere.

GRANDMOTHER: And the crickets hum like broken bells.

DRUM MAJOR: The smell of death!

Scene 23

The inn. People dance.

WOYZECK: *(enters the inn)* Dance! Dance! Everyone dance. Sweat and stink. He'll get you all in the end. *(sings repeat of Andres's song, "In the garden all day long")*

WOYZECK: *(to Margaret)* Come over here! Sit down. I'm hot. Whew. Hot. That's how it is. *(to Drum Major)* The devil takes one and lets the other go. You're hot Margaret. You'll be cold too someday. Look after yourself. Why don't you sing me something?

MARGARET: Down to the south
I will not stray.
For silken gowns
I do not yearn.

47

For pointed shoes
I do not yearn.
A servant girl must say her nay.

WOYZECK: No. No shoes. You can get to hell without shoes.

MARGARET: Oh no, my love the girl did moan. Just keep your money and sleep alone.

WOYZECK: Sleep alone. Wouldn't wanna get covered in blood.

MARGARET: What's that, on your hand?

WOYZECK: Where?

MARGARET: You're all red! Blood!

DRUM MAJOR: Is he bleeding?

WOYZECK: Blood? No.

FIRST JOURNEYMAN: Blood.

WOYZECK: Must have cut myself. Cut my hand.

FIRST JOURNEYMAN: *(pointing to elbow)* How did it get on there?

WOYZECK: When I wiped it off.

FIRST JOURNEYMAN: Wiped *that* hand on your elbow? Some trick.

GRANDMOTHER: And the giant said, "Fee fi fo fum. I smell, I smell, I smell human flesh."

WOYZECK: What do you want? Damn you! What do you know? Nothing! Do you think I've killed someone? Look at yourselves!

Scene 24

WOYZECK: The knife. Where's the knife. Here where I left it. Getting closer. Closer. Shhh. . . . Quiet! Shhh! Quiet. Something moved. Shhh. Over there. Marie? Aaahhh. Marie. Quiet. So quiet. You're so pale, Marie. What is this red thing around your neck? A necklace. Is that what he gave you to do it with him? Such a fat sin. Black sin. You were black with sin but I've made you white again. Your hair is a mess, Marie. Didn't comb it today. Let me tidy it for you. *(a sudden noise)* Something over there. Cold. Still wet. Got to go. Got to go. People!

Scene 25

WOYZECK: *(preparing to throw the knife into the water)* It will sink like a stone in the dark water. The moon is like a blade dipped in blood. *(starts to throw knife)* Aaah. *(Andres grabs his hand. Woyzeck is arrested, Marie removed.)*

Scene 26

As Woyzeck is being trussed and forced to his knees people speak as they surround him.

SHOWMAN: This is a human being. Put humanity to shame!

49

GRANDMOTHER: I smell human flesh.

FIRST JOURNEYMAN: Make a hole in your soul.

MARGARET: *(sings)* Down to the South I will not go.

SERGEANT: Give the man a hand, soldier.

DOCTOR: You're an interesting patient, Woyzeck.

CAPTAIN: A hair. A hair from somebody's beard.

PAWNBROKER: An economical death.

ANDRES: Can you hear it now, Woyzeck?

DRUM MAJOR: Try whistling now.

CAPTAIN: A good murder. A real murder.

DOCTOR: A beautiful murder.

CAPTAIN: As good a murder as you'd ever want to see.
We haven't had one like this for a long time.

(Child sings as she brings on the axe and presents it ritualistically to Andres)

CHILD: Nothing on this earth will last
All will fade
All will pass.

Scene 27

In court.

WOYZECK: Gentlemen, pity me. I am science. Every week I get two groschen for my scientific self. Don't break me apart or I'll go hungry. I am spinosa pericyclida. I have a Latin spine. Don't break me, don't break me.

(blackout, the sound of the axe that began the play)